The Lymington River is a small river in Hampshire, flowing through the New Forest into the Solent. The river has a total length of 22 kilometres (13.5 miles), although the initial part, north of Brockenhurst, is known as Highland Water. Highland Water rises north of the Ocknell Inclosure and flows for 10 kilometres (6 miles) to Bolderford Bridge where it meets the Ober Water.
It is here that Hugh and I have started as from then on it is known as the Lymington River and flows for a further 12 kilometres (7 miles).
It winds its way through some of the most glorious unspoiled parts of the New Forest. From Bolderford Bridge to Long Reach on the Plywell Marsh Nature Reserve, ending as it flows out into the Solent.

Hugh and I have walked most of the river and tried to capture some of its mysteries, some of the deeper and less well trodden paths. I tend to work out on site (Plein Air) with pastels and watercolour to capture the immediacy of the moment. Then, using those sketches either finish them back in the studio or use them as reference for larger canvases in oil or acrylic. Working outside helps me (I hope) capture an ephemeral, transient moment of light and time.
Hugh's work has its own timeless quality finding tranquillity in a silent part of the river, the majesty of a single tree or the menace of a storm about to break.

Just down river from Bolderord Bridge

September: We walked from the car park at the Balmer Lawn Hotel up river to Bolderford Bridge just over a kilometre I think (check) ? The sun was intermittent but strong when out, casting dappled light in the trees and allowing good strong reflections in the iron brown water.

From Bolderford Bridge
I wait for the sun to rise just high enough to kiss its morning light on the top of the trees

Following the first stretch takes us along Water Copse Inclosure, it is a thin deeply wooded strip between the New Park Hotel grounds and Black Knowl Heath. On the Heath the pigs and piglets were out for early pannage this year. Pigs are allowed out onto the open Forest during the "pannage" season, always in the autumn, in order to eat the acorns which could prove fatal to the ponies. Rooting by the pigs could cause damage to the Forest so they must be inspected and ringed, and a marking fee paid, before they are allowed onto the Crown lands.

Floods at Bolderford Bridge

The Pigs are out a Pannaging

At last sunlight, after days of rain - deep puddles on Black Knowl Heath

Oak tree mirrored in the flood water

From Bolderford Bridge the light cuts through a clearing, creating deep shadows on one side of the river and lights up the shallows on the left. The River is flooded and Hugh has gone just a bit up river following the Ober Water to capture the reflections of an old oak now stranded in a temporary lake. Further down stream on our return journey back along the river, the light was lower and came streaming through quite a dense patch of oak and birch.

There is plenty to paint here as the light ripples and dances on the shallow water, a place to return to over and over again I think, as the colours and the nature of the river will change with the seasons.

Along the edge of Watercopse inclosure as the sun goes down

Watercopse Inclosure

October and the first indications that our trek along the river would not be as easy as we thought.

Parked again near the Balmer Lawn Hotel, the bit of river next to the car park is known locally as Brockenhurst Beach. It's a very popular spot during summer, an easily accessible stretch of the river that everyone can enjoy. However you can't go down river from there as the land on either side is private. So we walked back along the A337 into Brockenhurst until we came to Bridge Farm and after explaining to Tim Cadbury what we were trying to do, he happily allowed us to walk along his stretch of land.

The river floods at the Balmerlawn car park

Looking across the river from Watercopse to Black Knowl Heath

The river bend just before the railway bridge

The light just catches the reed bank

Starting opposite the car park the river on Tim's land winds its way down stream until it disappears under the railway bridge.

So back to Bridge Farm and this time armed with sketch book, pastels and paints. Once again the weather was on our side but it was quite difficult keeping to the river's edge, fences to be climbed or scrambled under, boggy bits and ditches to be negotiated. It was a dark and secret part of the river with sunlight only spilling in occasionally. There were a few paths along the edge the further we went, possibly made by fishermen from the Welworthy fishing club who, I believe, still use that stretch.

Bright sunlight that occasionally touched the water giving glorious glimpses of the river

The Old Railway Bridge at Bridge Farm

The challenge is always to find something that captures that part of the river, so it took a few days to find, but finally on a river bend there were a couple of large lichen-covered trees leaning out, creating good reflections with the sun shining through the undergrowth and just enough sky reflecting blue in the water. A little further down, almost at the railway bridge, the sunlight broke through the trees and lit up a patch of reeds that were just glowing a deep rich early Autumn reddish brown. A more difficult composition to capture but worth the midge bites.

The river suddenly lights up, be quick to capture this but beware of the midges !!!

And finally, at the bridge itself, I wanted that in one of the paintings as a marker, if you like, of the end of that stretch of river.

Old Man of the Woods

Hugh is away. Dubai, Bombay, somewhere, who knows? We have had the first frost. There is a lot more colour in the trees and I am out looking for access to the other side of the bridge to continue from where we left off. So up Balmer Lawn Road to Ivy Wood car park and then walk back along to Mill Road, but no luck with access, everyone seems to be out and I can't get to the river without trespassing.

Start again and from Ivy Wood but go down river instead. This is more like it, the river is quite narrow here and takes on a different feel, rushing and tumbling, darker and more difficult to access with no real footpaths, but good glimpses of river through tangled trees.

The river is running quite fast here but the light is fantastic

Rope Swings in Ivy Wood

I like Ivy Wood, so back there today and a walk down stream. There are some interesting bends in the river and a thick carpet of leaves in the woods giving some glorious golden red browns to paint. Hugh is back for a few days but he has only just got home so I went out again on my own, not the best of days, not raining but a blanket of grey. Awful ! Tomorrow I will buy myself some wellies, I got a tad muddy.

Watercolour of Ivy Wood, no footpaths but the river reveals itself through the tangle

Reflections and Fallen Trees at Moors Corner

I want some sun, the Autumn colours are at their best but not for long, the wind is blowing the leaves off in drifts. Although the light was not too good it was a wonderful blustery walk with the wind everywhere kicking up little whirlwinds of leaves.

I walked for hours but did not get that far - lots of smaller streams and muddy ditches crossing my path and because of no wellies, too many detours to get far along the river. I walked up to where the river bends into Moors Corner.

Whirlwinds of falling Beech leaves on the edge of the river in Ivy Wood

Approaching Moors Corner

This is the first chance Hugh and I have had to go out since he got back from Dubai / Bombay. He has missed the best of the autumn colours (he's shooting Black and White so possibly not a problem) but today was a dry day. No rain. The sunlight was not the best, but worth a try, so we headed out to pick up the next bit of the river. Drove past Ivy Wood car park on the B3055 and parked up on the bend in the road at Perrywood Ironshill Inclosure. Walked down river to the fallen tree that I had came across earlier for a start, but then turned round and continued down stream into Baker's Copse and further into Highwood Copse.

Pastel and watercolour - The River at Baker's Copse

It is cold, too cold to do any sketches today, but I took a couple of photos that I hope will be worth working from.
I was wearing my NEW wellies today and just as well.

It looks like we might have to ask permission for the next bit of the river, will get on to that, but for now download the pics and see what's worth looking at and what, if anything, will make a good subject to paint. I hope Hugh has captured a shot or two or even just noted a couple of places worth a re-visit.

Note to self:
Must explore Setley Common, Newlands Copse and Roydon Woods.

Royden Woods >

Footbridge Royden Woods

The winter went on and on and according to the radio statistics the coldest for over 100 years. I re-visited and sketched and painted parts of the river we had already done, but have just been too cold to do anything worthwhile. It is time to give up and wait for some warm weather.

A lot later in Royden Woods we found ancient trees, Oak and Beech also moss covered banks that must have marked out now long forgotten boundaries. Rills and riverlets tumble down to meet the Lymington river that we are trying to follow. I have been told that the bluebells are spectacular but we have missed them this year.

Acrylic, Tangled up in Royden Woods

Old lock gates

My son Zak said he could meet us for the afternoon. It would be good if he can be included, if only briefly, in this project as he was a major part of " A YEAR IN THE NEW FOREST" a small book we put together in 2008/9.

Hugh and I drove past the pub (the Filly Inn) and turned into Sandy Down. We followed the road until it crossed the river and there we had a bit of luck, meeting up with a group af people who, as it turned out, were volunteers for the Hampshire and Isle of White Wildlife Trust (HIWWT). They were laying hedges at the woodland we wished to enter to go up river and we were not sure if this was private land or not.

After a brief conversation, we began to realise that this was going to be a tricky project as so much of the river bank is in private hands, or not accessable to the public. They told us that about a third of the river was owned and managed by the Trust and we would have to ask permission. We were given directions to meet up with Mark Boxall, the estate manager for this stretch. We could meet him somewhere on Roydon Lane where he was working. He was great. After we had explained what we wanted to do he made a couple of phone calls and we had permission to enter the Wildlife Trust's lands. Thank you ! Without that we would have had to stop right there and probably abandoned the project.

So, time for lunch. We met at the Filly Inn where Zak was waiting for us. After a pie and a pint it was back down to where Sandy Down crosses into Church Lane. We parked up, donned walking boots and........... the sun went in. Never mind. We were there and the river was flowing and not another soul could be seen in the woods. Zak is keen to be shooting out in the landscape again after months of Uni project work. I took some photos for reference but need to go back and draw. I thought the best place for me was on a gravel bank just past Trout Corner, a wide, curving, fast running part of the river with enough light coming in to allow some good reflections. I managed to do a quick indian ink drawing of an old lock gate and I eventually painted near sunset, a pollarded ash tree that was leaning out into the river.

The Hawthorn puts on a good show

Zak tied up with Uni work again and Hugh on a case in Germany, so I was on my own when I first visited Vicars Farm. A glass and silver jeweller, a wonderful lady called Jane Pit-Pitts, had invited us down to her part of the river. Some of her land runs along the edge of the Lymington River and connects onto The Reed Bed walk that is managed by the HIWWT. This stretch will take us all the way into Lymington but today is a little boggy. When I say 'a little' I mean knee-high and sinking over the top of my now well used wellies.

Hugh is back and Zak has a day off so we all head down there again while the sun is out.

Zak captures the Hawthorn in full bloom

Hugh down at Vicars Hill Farm, on his own. We almost lost him. He really did sink into the mud, nearly lost his camera and came back smelling of .....

The Reed Beds from Vicars Farm

Next is Bridge Road, Undershore, and then down river to the Plywell Nature Reserve and Long Reach where the river flows out into the Solent, and journey's end.

Golden Reeds Vicars Farm

Sunset over the Reeds at Undershore

The earliest settlement in the Lymington area was around the Iron Age hill fort known today as Buckland Rings. The hill and ditches of this fort still remain. Lymington itself began as an Anglo-Saxon village. The Jutes arrived in the 6th Century and founded a settlement called Limentun. The Old English word 'tun' means a farm or hamlet whilst limen is derived from the ancient British word 'lemanos' meaning elm tree.

In the pubs, the locals like to tell stories about its smuggling history; there are unproven stories that under the High Street are smugglers' tunnels that run from the old inns to the town quay.

Lower Quay Street

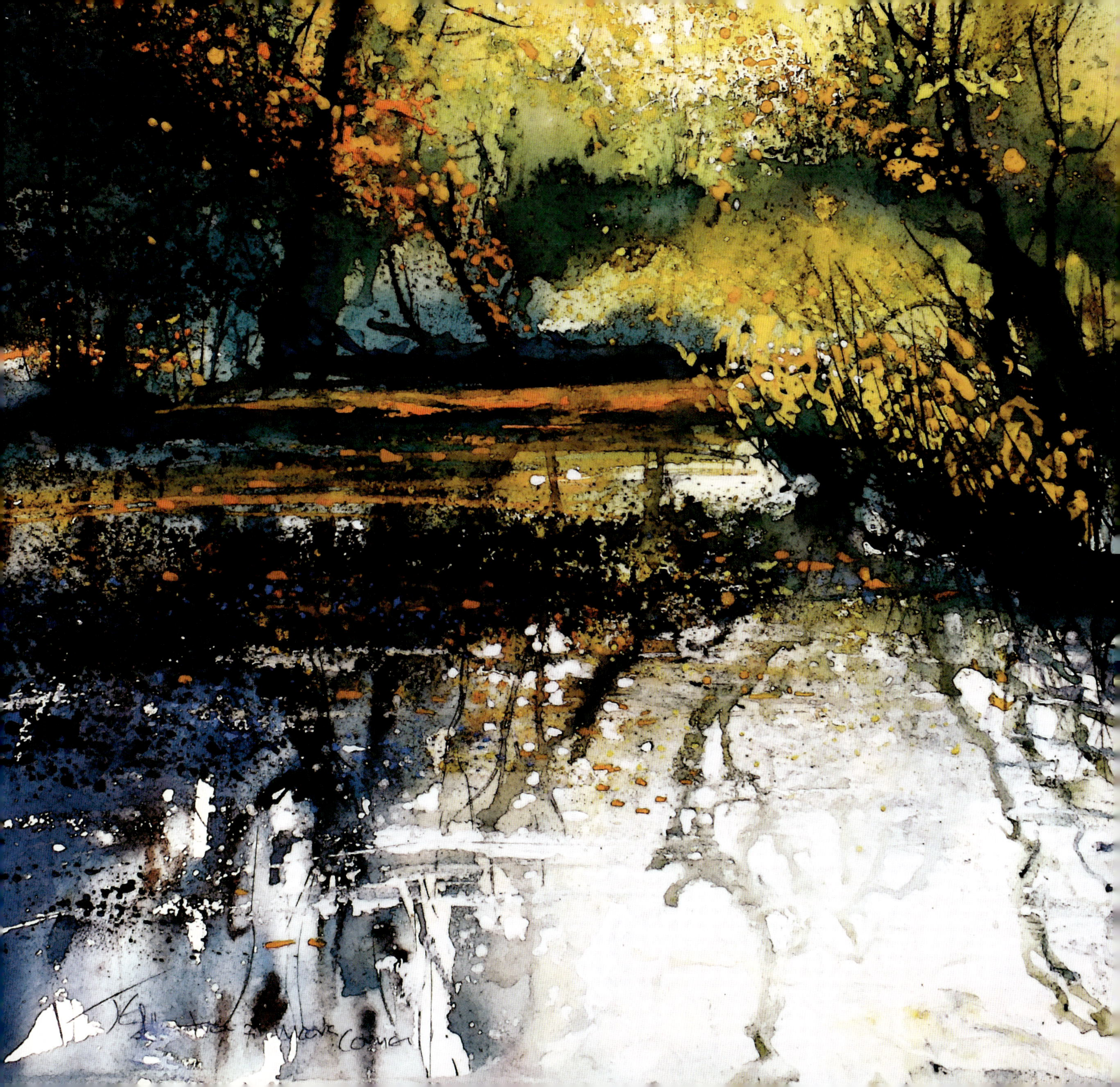

One of the great joys of creating a project like this is the discovery of places you might not necessarily have found. The walk along the shore from the end of Tanners Lane to Shotts Lane is one of those. We were trying to find a place to paint and photograph the end of the river, after it has left Lymington and flows out to the Solent. This stretch of shoreline looks out across the Plywell Nature Reserve with views of the Isle of Wight and The Needles in the distance. With bent, stark, windblown trees, mudflats and bleached white driftwood it has endless possibilities.

Plywell Lake

The windblown Trees at the end of Tanners Lane

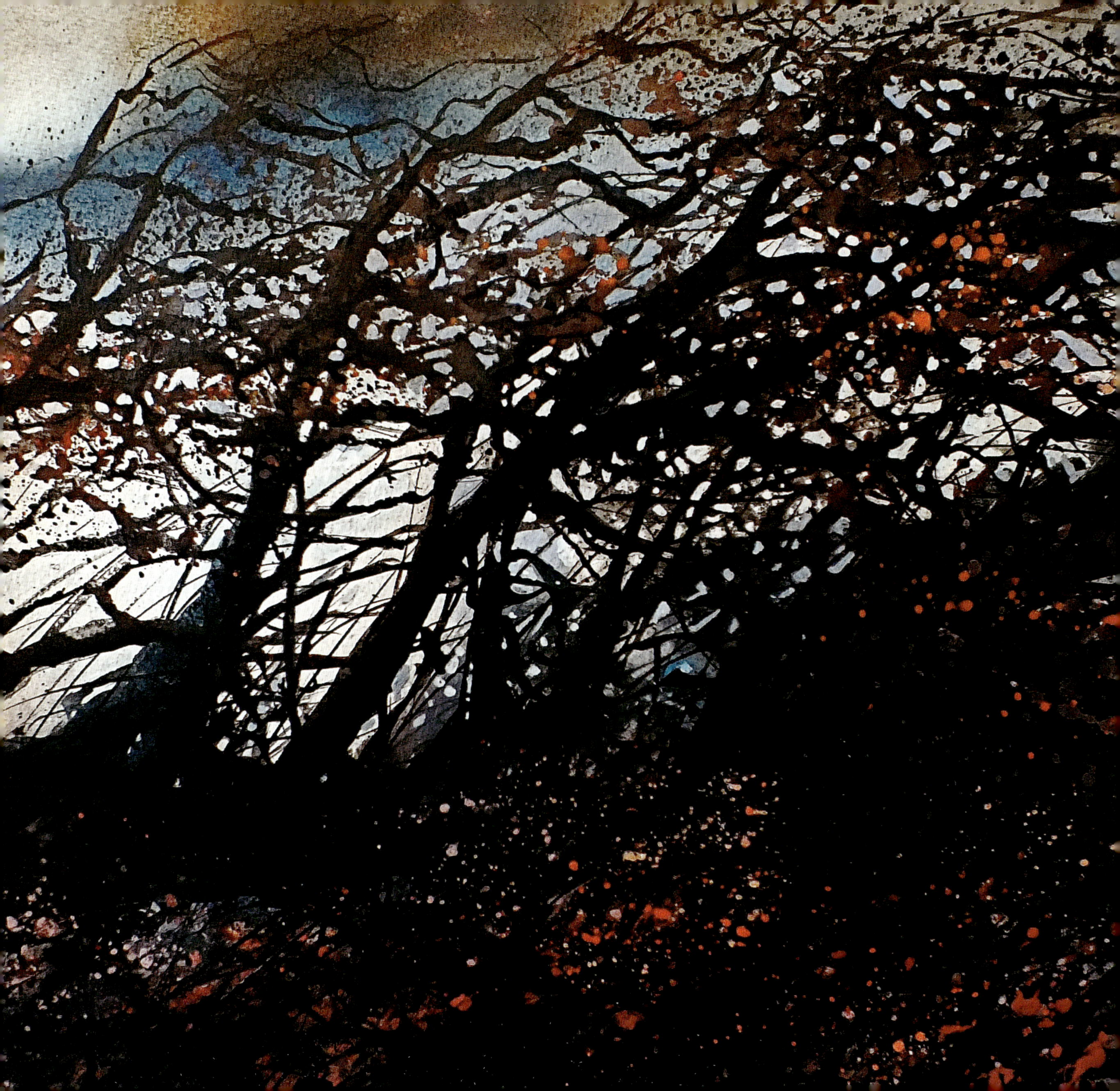

On the west side of the river on the edge of Lymington you can pick up the coastal path - The Solent Way. As it skirts Normandy Farm at Aden Bank there are some wonderful views across to Long Reach, the end of the river. The path then takes you on to Oxley Marsh and the Keyhaven Marshes where both Zak, Hugh and I have walked, painted and photographed. It is here that we end this book...... **except for the places in between.**

A wild and windy day on the Solent Way

One of those distractions - Hatchet Pond just before a storm

Oh Dear!

In between stumbling along (and in) the Lymington River with Pete, I frequently drive up to Turf Hill with or without the Wooden Spoon pub's black lab 'Boo'. Sometimes I take my Canon 7D. I then jog and walk around this beautiful part of the New Forest.

One misty morning, as I entered the wood by Millersford, I looked up to my left and was much taken by the soft light and delicate outline of trees that created a natural picture. Breathe out gently, then Click! Pleased with my effort I jogged on.

A bit more jogging and a few more pictures and I arrived back at my car, realising that I was getting a bit too old for this method of photography. My camera had definitely gained weight during the trek.

Later that day I downloaded the pictures to my Mac to see what I had got. Good grief! There was a deer in that first picture. I don't wear my glasses when taking pictures, but my eyesight can't be that bad surely? I suppose this is why I never took up wild life photography.

On a visit to Compton Acres I saw this and knew I had to paint it - Japanese Maple

Chasing the Snow

It was early evening and snow was falling gently. It was settling. I felt growing excitement at the prospect of getting some great snow scenes. So often in the recent past I had found myself deployed to foreign (semi tropical) locations to help sort out some problem or other. Caracas in January, Medellin in February or Manila are all snowless.

The snow started to melt. Finally, a couple of days later, I got out and took this picture in the Avon Valley. I am within 100 metres of the main Salisbury to Ringwood road. The glorious snow covered landscapes had disappeared. but there was just enough snow left to reveal the ploughing lines that created beautiful curving patterns in the earth. The truth is that you do not have to move far from civilisation to find beauty on the edge of the New Forest.

I painted this up on Beaulieu Heath when the wind was blowing a hoolie, totally insane really as it was very cold as well.
It's a pastel sketch and then over-painted in watercolour.

One of my favourite places at sunrise is up at Wild's Corner just inside the Godshill Inclosure This is Acrylic on canvas and about a metre sq.

Beaulieu to Buckler's Hard

The Beaulieu River forms part of the Beaulieu Estate. It is one of the very few private rivers in the world but is accessible by hiring a boat from Buckler's Hard. The banks of the river are rich in vegetation and wildlife. You cannot see much of the river at the start, but there is a delightful wood 'en route', and that is where this photo was taken.

Lost in the Woods, Beech, Oak, Ash, Holly, everything!

This little watercolour was done after finding the track that leads down to The Shallows behind Spinners Garden.

Spinners is a peaceful woodland garden overlooking the Lymington valley with a reputation for rare and unusual plants collected over the last fifty years.

The teazels - ink and wash

Hugh and Zak both photographed this old lock gate and I couldn't resist it either. I think it's the only one on the river, not used any more but covered in ivy and rust, it was a must, this sketch is in Indian ink.